Contents

✔ KU-526-712

1

Tudors Triumphant

King Henry VII of England. The king looks kindly in this portrait, but he was a shrewd and ruthless ruler.

At the battle of Bosworth Field, on 22 August 1485, the army led by Henry Tudor, Earl of Richmond, won the day. The loser, King Richard III, was killed in the fighting. One of Richmond's followers is said to have plucked the dead king's crown from a bush and placed it on the earl's head. Richard's naked corpse was slung across a horse and led away, while Richmond was hailed as the new king, Henry VII (1485–1509).

The battle of Bosworth ended the Wars of the Roses, a thirty-year struggle for the crown between two rival groups, the Lancastrians and the Yorkists. Of course, in 1485 no one could be sure that the wars were over. But many powerful and troublesome nobles had died in the fighting, and most people were so tired of war and uncertainty that they were happy to live under a strong king. Henry VII came to the throne at the right moment, but he also made the most of his opportunities. He tamed the nobility and made the monarchy rich and respected.

Henry's descendants – the Tudor kings and queens – kept an equally firm grip on power. They ruled through a period of tremendous changes and challenges, and several of the Tudors are still popular legends – notably 'Bluff King Hal' (Henry VIII), and 'Good Queen Bess' (Elizabeth I).

Henry VII [1485–1509]

Born in 1457, Henry was Welsh by birth. In 1471 he became the Lancastrian leader, claiming the English throne. He lived in exile while the Yorkist king Edward IV reigned. After defeating Edward's brother, Richard III, Henry became king and married Elizabeth of York to bring together the rival houses of Lancaster and York. By carefully supervising the nobility and building up his income (he personally checked every penny of the accounts) Henry made the monarchy strong and put Tudor rule on a firm foundation.

The Making of the United Kingdom 1500-1750

Crown and Parliament

Nathaniel Harris

WAYLAND

The Making of the United Kingdom 1500-1750

Church and People
Crown and Parliament
Social Change
Unification

Cover: Queen Elizabeth I, The Armada Portrait: (inset) The Gunpowder Plot conspirators.

Series and Book Editor: Rosemary Ashley
Designer: Joyce Chester

First published in 1996 by Wayland (Publishers) Limited, 61 Western Road, Hove, East Sussex, BN3 1JD, England.

British Library Cataloguing in Publication Data
Harris, Nathaniel, 1937–
  Crown and parliament. – (The making of the United Kingdom, 1500–1750)
  1.Great Britain – Politics and government – 1485– – Juvenile literature 2.Great Britain – History – Tudors, 1485–1603 – Juvenile literature 3.Great Britain – History – Stuarts, 1603–1714 – Juvenile literature
  I.Title
  941'.05

ISBN 0-7502-1812-6

Typeset by Joyce Chester
Printed and bound in Italy by G. Canale & C.S.p.A., Turin

Picture acknowledgements
The pictures is this book were supplied by: AKG London 14. Bridgeman Art Library 11, /cover (main picture), /Cheltenham Art Gallery & Museum 29, /Christies 4, /Guildhall Library, London 42, /Museum of London 32, 34, /Royal Naval College, Greenwich 43, /Scottish National Portrait Gallery 41, /Wallace Collection 22. Mary Evans Picture Library 7, 10, 12, 20, 21, 28, 37, 38 (both), 40, 41 (lower). Michael Holford/National Maritime Museum 16. Image Select 5, 6. Press Association/Topham 8. Visual Arts Library 9. Wayland Picture Library cover (inset), 13, 18, 19, 23, 24, 25, 26, 30 (top), 31, 33, 36, /National Maritime Museum 35, /National Portrait Gallery 13 (top), 17, 30 (lower), /Scottish National Gallery 15.

A. Cardinal Wolsey.
B. Warcham Archbishop of Canterbury.
C. Bishops.
D. Abbots.
E. Barons.
F. Prior of St John of Jerusalem
G. Earls.
H. Duke of Norfolk.
I. Duke of Suffolk.
K. Garter.

The House of Lords during the reign of Henry VIII. The King sits enthroned, with members of the House of Commons standing in a crowd, top right. On the left are the bishops and abbots who ran the monasteries. The picture shows the House of Lords before the monasteries were dissolved.

Tudor kings and queens governed England directly. They were helped by a Council whose members advised them on how the country should be governed and made sure that royal decisions were carried out. Councillors were chosen by the monarch, and might be men of ability from humble backgrounds. But the Council always included a number of powerful nobles as well. The Crown needed the support of these great landowners, but they were not allowed to dominate (control) the Council. One vital Tudor achievement was to turn the nobles into servants of the state under the monarch, not rivals for power.

Tudor parliaments

Parliament consisted of the Crown (monarch), the Lords and the Commons. The king or queen decided when and if to summon (call) Parliament, to prorogue (adjourn) it, or dissolve (end) it. The House of Lords consisted of peers and bishops, who were members by right of their titles. The Commons was elected, mainly by landowners in the counties and well-off citizens in the boroughs (towns). Most English people played no part in elections and had no say in how they were governed.

The House of Lords during the reign of Queen Elizabeth I. The throne is much grander and the Queen is more majestic than in Henry VIII's time.

One of the Tudors' most effective weapons was propaganda. At court, elaborate ceremonies were developed to make the monarch appear godlike, far above any noble in status. Writers were hired, and books and pamphlets were printed, to reach large numbers of people for the first time. The writers praised the monarch as the Lord's Anointed (appointed by God). They insisted that disobedience to the king was a sin, and pointed out the horrors of rebellion and civil war. And when Henry VIII became head of the Church (see page 9), the message was repeated every week from every pulpit.

Propaganda was important because the Tudors desperately needed popular support. Although they seemed powerful, they had very little force at their command. They could not afford a permanent army, but depended on the militia (a locally raised 'people's army'). There was no national police force or civil service. Rulers needed willing co-operation in government from the nobility, and also from the gentry. In fact local government was mainly carried out by the gentry, acting as justices of the peace (JPs). At every level, Tudor government was built on a partnership between the Crown and people with wealth and influence.

In law, too, English kings and queens were not absolute (all-powerful).

'For the King of England cannot alter nor change the laws of the realm at his pleasure,'

wrote the fifteenth-century lawyer Sir John Fortescue. But a monarch did have a range of special powers and privileges, such as the power to wage war or make peace. These special powers, known as the royal prerogative, made it possible to rule in normal times. But if new laws were needed, they had to be made by Parliament.

Parliament was an assembly of men from all over the country, who represented the wealthy community. Parliament brought together the Crown, the Lords (nobles and bishops) and the Commons. The Commons consisted of men chosen from the countryside (counties or shires) and the towns (boroughs). Members of Parliament (MPs) were mainly elected by landowners and well-off citizens, and consisted of royal ministers, minor nobles, gentry and merchants. The great mass of ordinary people had no say.

The House of Commons in 1656, during the Commonwealth (see pages 30–31). The Speaker sits enthroned, with the MPs all round him. They are not seated on separate benches, representing Government and Opposition, as they are today.

When the present queen, Elizabeth II, speaks from the throne, she is really announcing policies decided by her government – unlike Henry VIII and Elizabeth I in the pictures on pages 5 and 6. The ancient tradition shown in the pictures is still carried on: at the opening of Parliament the monarch addresses the Lords, while the Commons stand in a crowd at the door. Now, of course, the Commons are actually far more important than the Lords.

For hundreds of years to come, people with power, wealth and education claimed that they had the right to speak and decide for everybody.

A law was made by Parliament when the House of Lords, the House of Commons and the king or queen were all agreed on it. A proposed law was called a bill; a law that had been passed was known as an act or statute. Statute law was supreme, overriding any other type of law.

For most of the time, statutes were concerned with everyday matters. New laws were not needed very often, so monarchs might reign for years without calling Parliament. When they did, it was often for a different reason: to raise money. In normal times, a king was expected to 'live of his own' – meaning he should live on his income from crown lands and other traditional sources. But extra funds were needed for an 'extraordinary' (special) expense such as fighting a war. Then Parliament would be asked to grant a subsidy – a sum of money raised by taxation.

Laws and taxes were the keys to Parliament's future. Under Henry VII, Parliament's role was still a minor one. But that was to change in the course of the Tudor century.

2

The King in Parliament

Young, handsome and determined to win glory, Henry VIII (1509–47) was a very different character from his careful, penny-pinching father, Henry VII. Henry VIII left the day-to-day government of the realm to his chief minister, the energetic Cardinal Wolsey. But the King remained the master, and a ruthless one. For years he hoped to conquer France – an unrealistic policy, as England was not strong enough. Henry spent all his father's savings and had to ask Parliament for subsidies. English people were generally glad to support wars against old enemies such as France and Scotland, but Parliament could be pushed too far. In 1523 Wolsey's demand for the huge sum of £800,000 was met with a 'marvellous obstinate silence'.

Despite his need for money, Henry VIII did not call parliaments very often. But there was a dramatic change when the great crisis of his reign began. Henry had only one surviving child, the Princess Mary. Like most kings at that time, Henry wanted a male heir, and believed that a woman would not be able to rule properly. He had fallen in love with a lady at court, Anne Boleyn, and he convinced himself that his marriage to Katherine of Aragon was invalid (unlawful) because she had been the wife of his dead elder brother. But the Pope, in Rome, who was the head of the whole Catholic Church, was reluctant to end the marriage.

Growing impatient, Henry dismissed Wolsey because he had failed to get results, and put more and more pressure on the Pope. Finally, Henry threw off the Pope's authority altogether. In doing all this, he worked with the support of Parliament. The 'Reformation Parliament' sat for six years (1529–36) and passed a long series of laws. The climax was the Act of Supremacy (1534), which declared that the monarch – not the pope – was the true head of the Church in England.

A portrait of Henry VIII by Hans Holbein, a famous German artist who painted many members of the court. He painted the strong and handsome 'Bluff King Hal', but the king was also a cruel, merciless ruler.

This print shows Henry VIII triumphing over the Pope after he had declared himself Head of the Church in England. Until the 1530s England had been part of the international Catholic Church, with the Pope in Rome as its head. In this print Henry is trampling on Pope Clement VII.

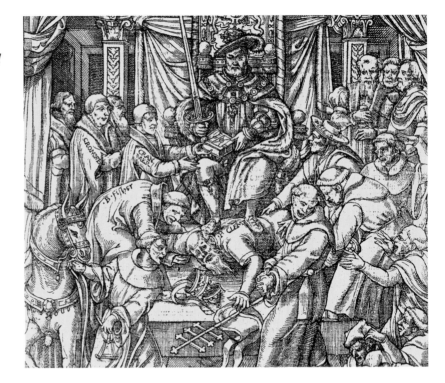

The Reformation crisis strengthened Parliament's position in the country. Although Henry himself complimented Parliament, saying

'we at no time stand so highly in our estate royal as in the time of parliament'.

Parliament was still under royal control. The King's ministers used all their influence to get their way, but most MPs were all too willing to co-operate. They were glad to see the Church lose many of its privileges, and shared Henry's wish for a settled succession to the throne after his death.

The succession

After twenty-three years of marriage to Katherine of Aragon, Henry VIII had fathered 'only' a daughter, the Princess Mary. He divorced Katherine and married Anne Boleyn. When Anne too gave birth to a daughter, Elizabeth (1533), and seemed unlikely to bear any more children, she was beheaded. In 1537 Henry's next wife, Jane Seymour, bore him the boy he wanted, Prince Edward. At Henry's death (another three wives later) he laid down the order of succession to the throne as 1. Edward, 2. Mary, 3. Elizabeth. The king's wishes were followed, and the English even agreed to have women rulers.

Parliament also passed the laws the King wanted for the Dissolution (closing down) of the Monasteries (1536–9). The monks were suspected of being more loyal to the Pope than to the King, and their riches were well worth plundering. As a result of the Dissolution, the King acquired vast lands which had belonged to the monasteries. Henry might have used such wealth to make himself an absolute ruler, above the law, but instead he waged expensive wars which forced him to sell many of his new properties. One important effect was that members of the landowning class, who bought the lands, became even stronger supporters of the king and the royal policy that had made them rich.

Henry's religious settlement – known as the 'Henrician Reformation' – transferred religious authority in England from the Pope to the King. But only limited changes were made in the doctrines and services of the Church. However, during the reign of Henry's son, the boy king Edward VI (1547–53), England became a Protestant country. Parliament dutifully passed the necessary laws.

A painting of an imaginary scene of the Tudor succession. It shows Henry VIII (centre) and his son Edward VI, holding a sword, Queen Mary and her husband Philip II of Spain (left); Queen Elizabeth (right, in front).

Lady Jane Grey

Jane Grey (1537–54) was the great-granddaughter of Henry VII. The sickly Edward VI was persuaded to alter the succession so that the Protestant Lady Jane would become queen rather than the Catholic Princess Mary. Jane was proclaimed queen on the death of Edward, but reigned for only ten days. Mary quickly rallied support and Jane was imprisoned in the Tower of London, and later executed.

When Edward died, loyalty to the Tudors brought Princess Mary to the throne (1553–8). As Henry VIII's eldest daughter she had a better claim than her Protestant rival, her cousin the sixteen-year-old Lady Jane Grey, who was beheaded. Mary was determined to restore Roman Catholicism. Parliament was still loyal and co-operative, especially once it became clear that the gentry who had bought monastery lands would not have to give them back.

Mary's policy of burning Protestants at the stake has given her a bad reputation. But in her own time the English probably blamed her more for her marriage to Philip II of Spain and an unpopular war with France. The war ended badly, with the loss of England's only continental outpost, Calais. Mary's reign finished in an atmosphere of gloom that made her sister and successor appear all the more dazzling.

Protestants being burned at the stake during the reign of Queen Mary. This print comes from a popular book of the time, Foxe's *Book of Martyrs, which told the stories of these persecuted Protestants, and encouraged great sympathy for them.*

3

A Queen under Pressure

Elizabeth (1558–1603) was probably the most idolized of all English monarchs. Adoration of the Queen was deliberately encouraged through poetry, paintings and pamphlets. But it was also based on the genuine popularity of the Tudors and Elizabeth's own personality and ability.

Elizabeth picked her advisers well. Leading councillors, such as her Secretary of State, William Cecil (Lord Burghley), were efficient, hard-working men. Important decisions were made in a small council – the Privy Council – rather than the larger, more time-wasting groups of the past. Among other things, the Privy Council managed Parliament so that laws went through smoothly and quickly, beginning with the establishment of a moderate Protestant Church.

The number of laws passed during Elizabeth's reign is impressive, since the Queen kept meetings of Parliament very brief. MPs were loyal to her and they were generous with subsidies, but even during the earlier years of her reign there was more plain speaking than there had been in the past. In particular, MPs urged the Queen to marry, and also to name her successor. However, Elizabeth sent vague but gracious messages and forbade further discussion about her marriage. When the topic came up again later, she grew angry, and told them

> *'I am your anointed queen and will never by violence be constrained [forced] to do anything.'*

Elizabeth was equally slippery when councillors and parliaments urged her to sign the death warrant of the imprisoned Mary, Queen of Scots, who had become the centre of Catholic plots against her. (Mary was finally executed in 1587.) When some MPs tried to discuss religious issues, Elizabeth was much fiercer, telling them not to

Queen Elizabeth I: young, beautiful, majestic. This was the only kind of portrait she allowed, right up to her old age.

William Cecil, Lord Burghley, was Elizabeth's able chief minister until his death in 1598.

Queen Elizabeth being carried through the streets, surrounded by her courtiers.

'intermeddle' with her prerogative. And MPs such as Peter Wentworth, who spoke up too freely about Parliament's liberties and privileges, were roughly handled.

The defeat of the Spanish Armada in 1588 was the high point of Elizabeth's reign, but not its end. After this great triumph things started to go wrong. England suffered from bad harvests, rising prices and plague, while the war against Spain dragged on miserably. Relations between Queen and Parliament became strained.

Peter Wentworth

Peter Wentworth (c.1530–1596) was an early champion of Parliament. He stood up boldly for Parliament's 'liberties and privileges'. In particular he defended its freedom of speech, denouncing attempts to prevent debates on topics such as religion and the succession. His activities earned him several spells in the Tower of London, where he died in 1596.

Mary, Queen of Scots

Mary Stuart (1542–87) was Queen of Scotland from babyhood. She had a claim to the English throne through her grandmother, who was the eldest daughter of Henry VII. As a child, Mary was married to the French king, Francis II. After his early death she returned to Scotland and married her cousin Lord Darnley, and later the Earl of Bothwell, even though many believed him to be Darnley's murderer. She was forced to abdicate in favour of her son (later James VI of Scotland) and in 1568 fled to England where she was imprisoned. Mary became the focus of Catholic plots against Elizabeth I and her involvement eventually led to her execution in 1587.

The execution of Mary, Queen of Scots at Fotheringhay Castle in Northamptonshire, on 8 February 1587. The headsman (executioner) is about to strike.

As early as 1589 a clash occurred when Parliament complained about purveyance. This was the well-established custom by which the Crown bought provisions at special low rates. It was unpopular, and often abused by greedy or dishonest suppliers. The Queen told Parliament not to interfere, because purveyance was part of the royal prerogative. But she avoided a serious dispute by promising to improve the system.

These clever tactics were typical of the Queen. Elizabeth seemed to be insisting on her prerogative while actually making a concession. She did the same when a harder struggle broke out over monopolies. These are exclusive rights to make, sell or export something; because nobody else is allowed to do the same, the monopolist can charge as much as he likes. Many monopolies, on articles ranging from salt to playing cards, were simply gifts given by the monarch to courtiers. Under pressure from Parliament in 1598, the Queen promised to look into the matter, but little had been done by the time a new parliament met three years later. Discontent grew so great that some MPs wished

The defeat of the Spanish Armada. English seamen in their faster, more manoeuvrable ships, did serious damage to the great Spanish galleons. The Spanish fleet was finally destroyed by storms on its way back to Spain.

to pass a law against monopolies, even though this would have meant challenging the royal prerogative. Once more the Queen avoided a crisis, this time by taking action against the worst abuses.

Parliaments meeting towards the end of Elizabeth's reign were not entirely dominated by conflicts. Among other things, an effort was made to tackle severe social problems by devising a 'welfare system'. And, towards the end of her reign, there was an atmosphere of harmony, when the Queen made her celebrated 'Golden Speech' to Parliament, praising her people and declaring that

> *'this I count the glory of my crown, that I have reigned with your loves'.*

However, a distinct shift had occurred in the relations between Crown and Parliament.

16

King James: Letting the Reins Slip

Elizabeth never named her successor, but during her last years her councillors were secretly in touch with her nearest relative, King James VI of Scotland. When the Queen died in 1603, the English crown passed without any problems to James. He became the first Stuart king of England, where he was known as James I (1603–25). England and Scotland now had the same king, but they remained separate countries.

A portrait of King James I of England and VI of Scotland, painted towards the end of his reign.

The new king was an odd, shambling figure, though he was also learned, humorous and sometimes very shrewd. James's unkingly personality was probably a disadvantage. So was his tendency to lecture Parliament on the God-given authority of kings (the Divine Right of Kings).

> *'The state of monarchy is the supremest thing on earth. For kings are not only God's lieutenants upon earth and sit upon God's throne, but even by God Himself they are called gods.'*

And, like God,

> *'they make and unmake their subjects. They have power of raising and casting down, of life and death, judges over all, and yet accountable to none but God only.'*

Such talk made Members of Parliament more anxious to guard their rights and James was often enraged by their stubbornness. MPs had become bolder even under Elizabeth, so any new, foreign monarch would probably have had difficulties. But James did make things worse by his rash speeches. And he was also wildly extravagant. A king was supposed to be 'bountiful', and his gift-giving could, for example, be used to win over troublesome MPs. But James too often handed out riches to handsome favourites such as George Villiers, whom he made Duke of Buckingham. Others – including MPs – were annoyed to see the Villiers family growing ever richer, and became even more annoyed when James then asked Parliament for money.

The crown would have been short of money even if James had been more careful. During the sixteenth century, rising prices had made it hard for the Tudors to manage on their traditional income. Queen Elizabeth was so careful that she was sometimes accused of meanness. She even saved some money – until the war with Spain began (in 1588). War was terribly expensive, and even Elizabeth got into debt. Royal lands were sold to pay the debts, but that only made matters worse: the next year, there was less money to come from rents. By the 1590s, Elizabeth needed frequent parliamentary subsidies to keep going. And under the Stuarts the situation was even worse.

The handsome George Villiers, Duke of Buckingham, was the favourite of James I, and later of James's son Charles I.

This meant that the Stuarts depended on Parliament much more than the Tudors had done. So Parliament gained a certain amount of power through its control of taxation. Parliament was able to ask for 'redress of grievances' (attention to complaints) before granting a subsidy, and if the king was desperate enough for money he had to agree.

MPs often grumbled that James should be able to 'live of his own' as his ancestors had done. But there was only one serious attempt to tackle the problem; the 'Great Contract' of 1610 would have scrapped some of the king's traditional rights in return for a fixed yearly income. But in the end, King and Parliament could not agree on the terms.

After this failure, James ruled without calling Parliament for eleven years, except briefly in 1614. His debts piled up, but he did find some new ways to raise money. Most of these were very unpopular, notably the sale of titles: knighthoods, baronetcies and even peerages were sold to anyone who could pay. This was a blow to the proud House of Lords. Until this time, the House of Commons had given James the most trouble, but from now on the House of Lords was also hard to handle.

'Gunpowder, treason and plot'

In 1605 Catholic plotters planned to destroy England's Protestant ruling class by blowing up King James and the assembled Houses of Parliament. The plot was revealed and Guy Fawkes and the other conspirators were executed. There had already been Catholic plots during Queen Elizabeth's reign, so the Gunpowder Plot confirmed most English people in a violent hatred of Catholics. In the Church of England, anyone who favoured elaborate ceremonies was suspected by Puritans of being a secret Catholic, and fear of 'popery' influenced English politics for over a century to come.

The arrest of Guy Fawkes on his way to blow up Parliament. Fawkes is the only Gunpowder plotter that most people remember now, but he was acting on orders from Robert Catesby and other Catholics in the North and was not the leader.

Francis Bacon (1561–1626) was a writer, scientist and philosopher as well as being James I's Lord Chancellor. When impeached in Parliament, he confessed to taking 'presents' (bribes). This was common practice with people in government at that time, but Bacon was convicted and disgraced.

James had even more problems with parliaments later on in his reign because of rivalries inside his court and council. One group would try to use Parliament to get rid of its rivals, not realizing that by doing this they were making Parliament stronger. Encouraged in this way, in 1621 the House of Commons impeached the Lord Chancellor, Francis Bacon, accusing him of taking bribes. Impeachment was a legal action in which the House of Commons accused a man and the House of Lords tried the case. Impeachment became one of Parliament's most powerful weapons against royal ministers and court favourites.

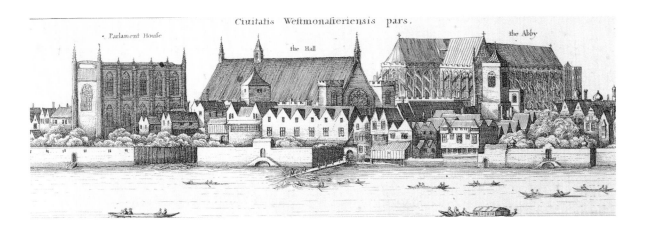

Ciuitatis Weftmonafteriensis pars.

Parliament Houfe ·   the Hall   the Abby

James had called Parliament in 1621 to ask for subsidies because there was a threat of war. Matters in Europe were very complicated, and the Commons began to discuss the situation. Like Queen Elizabeth earlier on, James told them that 'deep matters' of state were none of their business, and even claimed that he had the right to punish them.

> 'We [the king] *think ourselves very free and able to punish any man's misdemeanours in Parliament.*'

The Commons replied by writing a 'Protestation' into the Journal of the House, claiming that

> *the liberties ... and privileges of Parliament ... are the ancient and undoubted birthright and inheritance of the subjects of England; and that ... arduous and urgent affairs ... are proper subjects and matters of council and debate in Parliament; and that ... every Member of the House of Commons hath ... freedom of speech.*

They also insisted that an MP could not be arrested for anything done or said in the Commons. James's answer was to tear the page out of the Journal. Then he dissolved Parliament and imprisoned some of its leaders.

Three years later, James summoned another parliament. His son Charles and his favourite, the Duke of Buckingham, wanted war with Spain – so much, that they allied themselves with anti-Spanish MPs to force the king's hand. James is said to have told his son:

> 'You will live to have your belly full of parliaments .'

Westminster, in a seventeenth-century engraving, showing the Parliament House, Hall and Abbey. During this period, English monarchs lived not far away, at Whitehall. Both Westminster and Whitehall were still separate from London, which eventually grew and swallowed them up.

5
The Challenge to Charles

S mall, but handsome and dignified, Charles I (1625–49) was a more kingly figure than his father. But he was also less open and more obstinate. At a time when King and Parliament needed to meet each other half way and come to friendly arrangements, Charles was the wrong man in the wrong place.

A portrait of Charles I. The King was attractive and dignified, an art collector and a family man. But he was a bad politician. His mistakes cost him his throne and his head.

Charles I got off to a bad start. In May 1625, two months after becoming king, he married the French princess Henrietta Maria. This was unpopular because she was a foreign Catholic. He also followed a style of worship in the Church of England which many people thought was too much like 'popery'. Religion had played very little part in politics under James, but under Charles it complicated almost every dispute.

Charles's first parliament met in June 1625. It, too, got off to a bad start. Parliament voted only a small subsidy for war with Spain, and granted the King the right to charge customs duties, known as tunnage and poundage, for just one year. Parliament normally granted this right for a monarch's lifetime, so by doing this it was already declaring that it distrusted Charles, and was trying to make quite certain that he would have to call parliaments regularly when he needed more money.

In 1626 the King used a clever tactic to try to secure a friendlier parliament. He appointed leading opponents of the Crown, such as John Pym, as sheriffs – and sheriffs could not become MPs! But the new parliamentary leader, Sir John Eliot, was also a determined, fiery figure, and relations were no better than before. When Parliament decided to impeach the King's favourite, the Duke of Buckingham, Charles dissolved Parliament.

Needing money, Charles now raised it through forced loans and 'benevolences'. Benevolences were 'gifts' that, like the loans, were really compulsory. Earlier rulers had also raised them, usually with the excuse that the money was needed in an emergency. But they were never popular, and many people believed they were illegal. Charles also tried to establish that the monarch could imprison people 'for reasons of state'. But times had changed, and in 1628 Charles's third parliament passed a bill called the Petition of Right, declaring that benevolences were illegal and that no one should be imprisoned except for known offences. Charles realized that he would get no subsidies unless he signed the Petition and it became law.

Soon afterwards the unpopular Buckingham was assassinated. His death ought to have removed an obstacle to friendly relations between King and Parliament. But when

John Pym (1584–1643) held together the parliamentary opposition to Charles I and was one of the five members whom Charles attempted to arrest in January 1642 (see page 26). During the Civil War, 'King Pym' was the driving force in Parliament until his death in 1643.

John Pym was MP for Tavistock in Devon from 1624 until his death.

Parliament met again in January 1629, disagreements were more violent than ever. Charles had carried on collecting tunnage and poundage, insisting that it was his right. This sparked a debate so violent that the Speaker – still an officer of the Crown – decided to adjourn the proceedings. Since the Commons could only meet when the Speaker was present, MPs held him down in his chair. Meanwhile Eliot put on record a series of resolutions (declarations) that condemned changes in religion as well as charging or paying tunnage and poundage. The King immediately dissolved Parliament and imprisoned nine leading MPs, including Eliot, who died in the Tower in 1632.

Unable to work with Parliament, Charles made up his mind to rule without it. He managed to pay his way – just – by economizing, and also by reclaiming forgotten royal rights, or expanding some existing ones. The most celebrated example was Ship Money, a tax levied on coastal counties to keep the ships of the navy in good repair. Charles's decision to extend Ship Money to the inland counties, though disputed, brought him much-needed funds.

Charles's 'personal rule' lasted for eleven years (1629–40). They were years of peace, in which England stayed out of the war raging in Europe. One reason for this peaceful policy was that Charles could not afford a heavy extra expense such as fighting a war. But when he tried to force a

Religious quarrels complicated relations between Crown and Parliament, and caused division among parliamentarians during and after the Civil War. This print contrasts orderly churchgoers, listening to the 'orthodox true minister', with crowds out in the open, listening to the 'false prophet' – meaning a preacher who did not belong to the Church of England.

Thomas Wentworth, Earl of Strafford (1593–1641), was Charles I's chief adviser. His attempts to increase royal authority earned him the nickname 'Black Tom Tyrant'. He was condemned by the Long Parliament and was beheaded.

The beheading of the Earl of Strafford, outside the Tower of London on 12 May 1641. A crowd of 200,000 watched his execution.

new religious policy on Scotland, it sparked off a Scottish revolt. Charles's army was beaten, and he was left bankrupt and unable to pay off the victorious Scots.

Charles now had to ask Parliament for money. The 'Long Parliament' met in November 1640 and insisted that the King must accept its demands, including the execution of his chief adviser, the Earl of Strafford. Charles had to sign away Strafford's life. He agreed to the abolition of Ship Money and the special prerogative courts of Star Chamber and High Commission, which the Crown had used to enforce its policies. Acts were passed stating that Parliament must be summoned at least once every three years, and that the Long Parliament would sit as long as its members chose (it was finally dissolved in 1660).

W illiam Laud (1573–1645), Archbishop of Canterbury from 1633. The Puritans disapproved of his use of rites and ceremonies in religious worship, but it was favoured by Charles I. Laud tried to impose his 'Laudian church' on England, persecuting Puritans. His attempts to impose his policies in Scotland were even more disastrous and led to rebellion. He was accused, condemned by the Long Parliament and executed.

A satirical print showing the execution of Archbishop Laud.

Until this time, Parliament had claimed to be defending its ancient rights. But the Long Parliament, distrusting the King, was obviously altering the whole system of government. Some MPs began to be alarmed, and when radical religious changes were proposed, many members felt that things were going too far. A group began to form in support of Charles, to defend the constitution and the Church.

Some kind of solution might yet have been found. But then a Catholic revolt broke out in Ireland, accompanied by rumours of hideous massacres. A force had to be raised to put down the revolt, but who was to lead it? The King was always the commander-in-chief – but could he be trusted? Most MPs thought that if Charles had an army he might turn it against them. So, led by John Pym, they drew up a document called the Grand Remonstrance, which summarized Charles's misdeeds, and a Militia Bill to place the army under the control of Parliament. Charles denounced this revolutionary move, but then in January 1642 he put himself in the wrong by a bungled attempt to seize five MPs in the House of Commons. From then onwards, talks achieved nothing. The royalist MPs abandoned Parliament to join the King; his opponents remained in control in London. Both sides armed, and the Civil War began.

6
'The World Turned Upside Down'

The final result of the Civil War may not have been a certainty, but Parliament did start with important advantages. Roughly speaking, the King controlled the north and west, while Parliament commanded the south-east, which was the most prosperous area. Parliament was already used to doing business through committees, and governed quite efficiently. Parliamentary taxes were actually much heavier than anything levied by Charles I in the past. But Parliament's ability to raise money for the war helped to bring about its eventual victory. The Scots also came in on the side of Parliament. After almost two years of war, the battles of Marston Moor (1644) and Naseby (1645) decided the conflict, and soon the King was a prisoner.

Maps showing the areas held by royalists and parliamentarians during the Civil War.

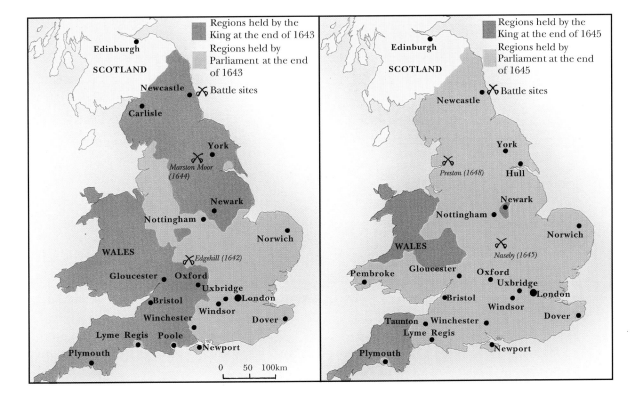

27

An episode in the Civil War showing Prince Rupert, a dashing royalist general, demanding the surrender of Leicester at the end of a victorious siege in May 1645.

But the basic problem – the fate of the King himself – remained unresolved. Most parliamentary supporters had never considered abolishing the monarchy. Somehow Charles must remain king and yet be kept firmly in check. Talks began between Parliament and King. But now there was a third political force – the victorious army, under leaders such as Oliver Cromwell (1599–1658).

Cavaliers and roundheads

The two sides in the Civil War were the royalists and the parliamentarians. The royalists were often called 'Cavaliers', which was originally an insult, meaning that the royalists were playboys. Similarly 'Roundheads', often used for the parliamentarians, described the short-haired London apprentices who rioted in support of Parliament. In reality, most royalists and parliamentarians dressed and looked very much alike.

Charles willingly joined in talks. But he was only playing for time while he made a secret agreement with the Scots. In 1648 royalist risings and a Scots invasion of England sparked off the Second Civil War. But Cromwell's army was victorious and demanded vengeance. When Parliament tried to continue talks with the King, the army chiefs sent Colonel Pride to throw out most of the MPs, an action known as 'Pride's Purge'.

Charles was put on trial, convicted of treason against his people, and beheaded on 30 January 1649. In his final speech, he claimed to stand for the people's 'liberty and freedom'. But he said

> *'I must tell you their liberty and freedom consists in having of government ... It is not for having a share in government ... A subject and a sovereign are clear different things.'*

The Battle of Marston Moor, 1644, *painted in the nineteenth century. The shattering defeat of the royalist army at this battle and at Naseby in 1645, made eventual victory by Parliament forces certain.*

King Charles I prepares for his execution. It took place on a well-guarded platform set up outside the Banqueting Hall of the royal palace in Whitehall, on 30 January 1649.

A portrait of Oliver Cromwell painted in 1649, just before his final victories over Scotland and Ireland.

Meanwhile England became a republic, known as the Commonwealth. The House of Lords was abolished, and power was shared between a Council of State and what remained of the Long Parliament after 'Pride's Purge'; this assembly became known as the 'Rump Parliament'.

The Commonwealth made enemies of royalists, moderate supporters of Parliament and many Puritans. The republicans themselves were divided over political, religious and other issues. So the Commonwealth's survival depended on the army; and the army always backed its outstanding leader, Oliver Cromwell.

In 1649–51 Cromwell crushed the final royalist effort and subdued Ireland and Scotland. In April 1653 he took power in England, getting rid of the Rump Parliament. Cromwell belonged to a small religious group, the Independents, and he tried to pick a Parliament consisting of men who were similar to himself:

> *'People chosen by God to do His work and to show forth His praise.'*

But he was unable to work with them. Then he was named Lord Protector, although many republicans were dismayed by this return to 'government by a single person'. And in fact Cromwell's difficulties with Parliament were not so very different from those of Charles I. For a time he

30

Be gone; you request.
You have Sett long enough

returned to direct military rule. Finally, in 1657, he accepted new proposals that made him a king in all but name. However, the first parliament under these new arrangements still attacked 'rule by a single person', and Cromwell soon dissolved it.

Cromwell turns out the members of the Rump Parliament, 1653. The artist who made this print has treated the event as a joke.

Perhaps, if he had lived longer, Cromwell would have won over the country gentry and set up a stable government. But when he died in September 1658, the Commonwealth quickly fell apart. The new Lord Protector, Cromwell's son Richard, quit, and civil war threatened. General Monck, commanding a parliamentary army in Scotland, marched south and took control. Monck summoned the surviving members of the Long Parliament, which authorized free elections. He invited the exiled Prince Charles (Charles I's son) to return after first obtaining attractive promises from him (the Declaration of Breda). And on 1 May 1660 the new parliament passed a resolution that

> 'the government was and ought to be by King, Lords and Commons.'

The prince returned to England as King Charles II, and the Restoration period began.

7

Royalty Restored

The coronation procession of Charles II, 1661, winding its way through triumphal arches from the Tower of London to Westminster. After so many changes and alarms in the 1650s, people were glad to have a king again.

The restoration of Charles II was greeted with joy by many former opponents of Charles I as well as by royalists. The events of the Commonwealth had shaken the landowning classes. Such people normally held authority in their own localities, but under the republic they found themselves ordered about by army officers and low-born officials, and had been forced to pay heavy taxes. They had also seen that unsettled times encouraged groups with disturbing, democratic ideas, such as the Levellers, who challenged their right to rule.

These disturbing events resulted in increased support for both the monarchy and the Church of England. Squire and parson – the country gentleman and the clergyman he appointed – became allies and also supported the bishops and the Crown. Bitter memories of the Commonwealth affected even those who later opposed the King, making them unwilling to risk a new civil war.

At the beginning of Charles II's reign, support for the monarchy was at its height. Elections returned a 'Cavalier Parliament'. The army was disbanded and the regicides (the men who had signed Charles I's death-warrant) were executed. Although Charles favoured tolerance, Parliament passed a series of acts punishing Protestants who could not accept the Church of England. Like Catholics, these Protestant 'Dissenters' were no longer allowed to hold any public office, whether that meant serving as a Justice of the Peace or a Member of Parliament or teaching at a university.

With the Church of England and the Cavalier Parliament supporting him, Charles II seemed to be in a strong position. The laws passed in 1641, limiting the prerogative (see page 25), had been passed by a properly elected parliament and remained in force. But royal rights that had been under threat before the Civil War were again accepted. The King still appointed ministers, made foreign policy and controlled the militia. And although he was supposed to summon Parliament at least every three years, he could still call, adjourn or dissolve it whenever he chose.

In practice Parliament met often under Charles II. The King was short of money, and like James I he was easy to blame because of his personal extravagance. Despite their loyalty, MPs criticized Charles and were reluctant to increase taxes. The early years of Charles's reign were marked by a series of disasters, notably the Great Plague (1665), the Fire of London (1666), and a badly conducted Dutch War (1665–67).

Charles II touching people to cure them of illness. Since the monarch was believed to be appointed by God, people thought his touch might cure their diseases.

During the middle years of his reign, Charles adopted a dangerous policy. Going behind the backs of most of his ministers, he made an alliance with Louis XIV of France. He received regular sums of money from the French king, and even agreed that he would eventually become a Roman Catholic. Yet most English people were fanatically anti-Catholic, and it was becoming clear that Louis, the all-powerful and Catholic 'Sun King', was aiming to dominate Europe. In English minds, 'France, popery and absolutism' (unrestricted power) became strongly linked for years to come. There were already some people who wondered about Charles's loyalties. But public concern grew greater when Charles's brother James – who was also his heir – admitted that he had actually become a Catholic.

Then in 1678 the storm broke. A 'Popish Plot' to murder Protestants and put James on the throne was revealed. The plot was mostly lies, made up by a rascal named Titus Oates. But fear swept the country. Then a disgruntled civil servant 'leaked' the latest round of talks between Charles's chief minister, the Earl of Danby, and Louis XIV. An angry House of Commons impeached Danby, and Charles was forced to dissolve the Cavalier Parliament.

The Great Fire of London, 1666, *painted by a Dutch artist. The fire burned for four days, destroying eighty-seven churches and over 13,000 homes.*

The main political issue was now whether the Catholic James could be allowed to become king when Charles died. Although Charles might have agreed to limit his brother's future powers, he was determined that the rightful heir should succeed him. But Charles's next parliament voted by a large majority to exclude (keep out) James from the throne. Charles dissolved Parliament but the crisis went on through two more parliaments, lasting until 1681.

For Parliament to change the royal succession was a revolutionary proposal. Supporters of Church and King were outraged, and began to meet and organize themselves as a political group. They became known as Tories. The other side, favouring James's exclusion, became known as Whigs. These are generally considered to be the first true political parties, arguing their cases in pamphlets and petitions and vigorously contesting parliamentary elections.

A painting of a sea battle between Dutch and English fleets, which took place in the English Channel during the war of 1665–7 (see page 33).

Charles II [1660–85]

Born in 1630, Charles was nineteen when his father, Charles I, was executed. He lived in exile until the Restoration in 1660. Remembered as 'the Merry Monarch', he was determined to enjoy himself, and spent huge amounts on his numerous mistresses and fourteen illegitimate children. Politically Charles admired the grand style of France's all-powerful Catholic monarch, Louis XIV. But he was also determined not to 'go on his travels' (into exile) again. In difficult situations he bowed to pressure, biding his time. Finally successful, his reign was a striking contrast to his father's.

Charles II was welcomed back to a country exhausted by war. At his death he left the monarchy strong.

After two more elections the Whigs kept their position as the biggest party in Parliament. But Charles stayed calm, cutting short parliamentary sessions while waiting for the tide to turn. Fortunately for him he was no longer short of money, since reform of the tax system and England's booming trade had greatly increased the amounts brought in by customs duties. Charles waited while his opponents became more and more impatient. Finally, in March 1681, MPs rode, armed, to a parliament at Oxford. A new bill to exclude James was passed, and yet again Charles ordered a dissolution. When it came to the point, no one wanted a new civil war, and the MPs tamely went home.

With opinion swinging in his favour, Charles took action. Now in partnership with the Tories, he further strengthened the Church of England. He changed the charters stating the rights of the leading towns, turning out the Whigs and replacing them with his own supporters. The Whig leader, the Earl of Shaftesbury, fled to Holland. Other leading Whigs were executed, charged with plotting against the King's life. In his final years, popular and free of parliaments, Charles ll's position was strong and secure.

8

The Glorious Revolution

Charles II died in February 1685. His brother James inherited a strong monarchy and, despite his Catholicism, a loyal people. Parliament was generous with funds, and a rebellion in the West of England, led by Charles's illegitimate son, the Duke of Monmouth, was a dismal failure.

However, after less than four years James II (1685–8) had squandered all his advantages by rashly promoting his fellow-Catholics. Possibly he only wanted to secure equal rights for them, although in the 1680s even that was an unpopular idea. But to many it seemed that he had more sinister intentions. Large numbers of Catholics were given positions in the army and in central and local government. The situation seemed all the more threatening because, across the Channel, the French king Louis XIV had begun a cruel persecution of Protestants.

The English hatred of Roman Catholics can be seen in this satirical print. It shows a procession of people leading clergy, bishops and the Pope to a bonfire. Behind the Pope, as he is drawn along (bottom right), stands the devil – 'the Pope's friend'.

Mary of Modena, James II's queen, flees from England with her baby son in 1688.

All this raised the old fears of 'popery and absolutism'. Although there were laws against Catholics holding office, James claimed that he could use his prerogative to suspend them. The laws were not cancelled, but they no longer operated. But if James could do this, the monarch was more important than the law, and Parliament would count for very little. So James's policy was seen as a political as well as a religious threat.

The King pressed on. In 1687 he tried to find allies among the Dissenters (Protestants who were not members of the Church of England) by issuing a Declaration of Indulgence. This suspended the laws against both Dissenters and Catholics. The Archbishop of Canterbury and six bishops refused to publish the Declaration in their churches, saying they believed James's use of the prerogative was illegal. James sent them to the Tower of London and later put them on trial. Other opponents of the King's policies, including government ministers, JPs and university teachers, were thrown out of office.

By this time James had made an enemy of almost every influential group. But Tories believed that it was their duty to obey the King, whatever he did. Their support for him was made easier because he was not young, and would be succeeded by Mary, his Protestant elder daughter by his first marriage.

William of Orange lands at Torbay in Devon on 5 November 1688. Although he claimed to have come to defend Protestant rights, James II's flight left the throne conveniently vacant.

Then, unexpectedly, James's second wife gave birth to a son. Now the heir to the throne would be brought up as a Catholic. This was too much even for the Tories. Leading figures from both the political parties secretly contacted James's son-in-law, the Dutch Prince William of Orange, and asked for his help. In November 1688, William landed at Torbay in Devon and advanced slowly towards London. When James's supporters began to desert him, he lost his nerve and fled to France, and Parliament offered the throne to William and his wife Mary. She was James's heir (apart from his little son), but she and William were to reign jointly, and after Mary's death in 1694 William ruled as king on his own. This was no longer rule by Divine Right. In effect, Parliament had appointed the sovereigns.

The events of 1688 became known as 'the Glorious Revolution'. This revolution was bloodless. It confirmed parliamentary liberties, and it marked a new beginning in the relationship between Crown and Parliament.

After the Glorious Revolution a Bill of Rights re-stated the liberties threatened by James II.

Bill of Rights

Some of the statements included in the Bill were:

'That the pretended power of suspending laws ... is illegal.

'That the pretended power of dispensing with laws ... is illegal.

'That levying money ... by pretence of prerogative without the consent of Parliament ... is illegal.

'That the raising or keeping a standing army within the kingdom in time of peace unless it be with the consent of Parliament is against the law.

'That election of Members of Parliament ought to be free.

'That freedom of speech and debates or proceedings in Parliament ought not to be ... questioned ...

'That for redress of all grievances and for the amending, strengthening and preserving of the laws, Parliament ought to be held frequently."

9

A New Kind of Partnership

After the fall of James II, the 'Revolution Settlement' arranged the nation's political affairs. A famous Bill of Rights re-stated English liberties: Parliament was the supreme law-making body; the royal prerogative could not be used to suspend laws or raise taxes; a Roman Catholic could not inherit the throne.

Other Acts were also important. Royal authority over the army had to be reconfirmed every year by a Mutiny Act passed by Parliament. A Toleration Act allowed Dissenters to worship in public. In 1694 a Triennial Act laid down that Parliament must be called at least once every three years, and could not sit for longer than three years.

Parliament had no means of making sure these Acts were obeyed, so a determined monarch might still have got round most of them. But William's main interest was not English politics. He wanted to save his native Holland from Louis XIV and to organize a 'grand alliance' to prevent France from dominating Europe. William allowed Parliament to play an important part in affairs, because that was

William III and Mary as king and queen, 1689. Traditionally, Mary alone should have ruled, with William as only her consort. Instead they became joint rulers, so that William remained king after Mary's death in 1694.

The Jacobite rebellions

Even though James II was exiled in 1688, he continued to claim the throne. So, later, did his son James, known as the Old Pretender (claimant), who was regarded by his supporters as King James III. These supporters were known as Jacobites – Jacobus is Latin for James. The Jacobites, relying on the loyalty of many Scottish Highlanders, made two serious attempts to overthrow the Hanoverian kings. In 1715 the Old Pretender landed in Scotland to lead an uprising, but it fizzled out. His son Charles Edward, the Young Pretender, 'Bonnie Prince Charlie', was more successful. In 1745 he landed in Scotland and led an army of Highlanders as far south as Derby, but there were no uprisings to support him in England and he was forced to turn back. He was crushingly defeated at the battle of Culloden in 1746, and escaped to France.

A portrait of 'Bonnie Prince Charlie' (1720–88). After his defeat at Culloden in 1746 he spent the rest of his life in exile.

the best way of keeping England in the alliance. And since King Louis was supporting the exiled James II, France was Parliament's enemy too. James was still a real threat, and in 1689–91 William sent forces to subdue the Jacobites (James's followers) in Scotland and Ireland.

'King William's War' against France lasted from 1689 to 1697. Then, in 1702, war with France broke out again. The cost of this long conflict had a great impact on Crown and Parliament. The House of Commons had once believed that Charles II could live on £1,200,000 a year. Now it recognized that William must have at least £5 million a year for government, war and diplomacy. A realistic tax system was developed, and modern government finance began with the founding of the Bank of England in 1694.

The Crown was strengthened, but now it governed in partnership with Parliament. Out of taxation William received a relatively small sum for his household expenses. This was called the Civil List. All the rest was for government spending, which MPs were entitled to investigate and check. Parliament met every year, and for longer periods of

William III at the Battle of the Boyne, 3 July 1690. The Catholics in Ireland had rebelled in support of James II, but were defeated by William and James fled.

The Bank of England was founded in 1694 when a company of merchants in London lent £1,200,000 to the government in return for certain privileges. This led to the bank becoming closely involved in government finances.

the year, and was involved in most government operations. As MPs gained experience, they understood government better and played their part sensibly. Parliament now became a permanent partner in government.

Political parties also became a regular feature of British life. Under William and Mary and Mary's sister Anne, political clubs developed, and newspapers, freed from censorship, brought politics to a wider public. But governments were not yet based on political parties. William refused to favour either Whigs or Tories, although he relied on the Whigs more because they were firmly in favour of the war with France. The same was true of Queen Anne (r.1702–14) until about 1710, when she began to share the Tories' wish for peace. But she always made the party men, whether Whig or Tory, work with non-party leaders whom she chose, such as the wartime Lord Treasurer, Sidney Godolphin. And a later non-party man, Robert Harley, finally brought to an end the French Wars in 1713 by signing the Peace of Utrecht.

As well as the war, Anne's reign saw the successful union of England and Scotland (1707). The other main issues were still religion and the succession. The 1701 Act of Succession barred Roman Catholics from the throne, but many Tories remained uneasy about the justice of taking the throne away from James II and his heirs, feeling that it was not right to interfere with the law of inheritance. By contrast, the Whigs were fully in favour of the Protestant succession.

The House of Hanover

After the 'Glorious Revolution' of 1688 Parliament declared that no Catholic could be crowned king or queen of Britain. James II and his son were therefore barred from the throne. James's Protestant daughters, Mary and Anne, reigned in turn and after Anne's death the crown went to Anne's nearest Protestant relative. This was a descendant of James I's daughter Elizabeth (sister of Charles I). Elizabeth's daughter Sophia had married the Elector of the small German state of Hanover. Sophia died a few weeks before Queen Anne, and so her son George inherited the British crown, becoming King George I.

George I, the first Hanoverian king. This picture is part of the decorations in the Painted Hall at Greenwich Palace, London (now part of the Royal Naval College).

Despite rumours and alarms, when Anne died, childless, in 1714 the Elector (reigning prince) of Hanover, a small German state, became George I of Great Britain, the first of the Hanoverian dynasty. Understandably the new king detested the Tories because of their divided loyalties, and relied on the Whigs. His lack of English and ignorance of the nation he had come to rule meant that the Whigs became even stronger. The first party-dominated ministries were formed and Tories were everywhere turned out of office. The Whigs, using the influence of the Crown to help them, won the 1715 general election and every election for decades afterwards.

Government during the early years of George's reign was confused by squabbles among the Whigs. But from 1721 the government was firmly under the control of Sir Robert Walpole (1676–1745), who remained in office until 1742. Walpole is often described as the first prime minister, because he could normally rely on the support of a majority in the House of Commons. This was done by skilful management of the Commons, and in particular by patronage – securing MPs' loyalty by distributing pensions, 'places' (profitable positions) and other favours.

Sir Robert Walpole addressing the Cabinet (the most important government ministers). The picture suggests that he was very much the man in charge. This was true, since Walpole alone enjoyed the King's confidence as well as controlling the House of Commons. This is why he has so often been called 'the first British prime minister'.

Walpole and later eighteenth-century prime ministers were still chosen by the king and depended on his favour. In 1727, when George I died, Walpole was prepared to resign at once because he knew that George II disliked him (but George changed his mind!). However, although the king still chose his chief minister, he had to pick someone who could get his business done in Parliament – in other words, someone who could put together a parliamentary majority. Ministers were still royal ministers, but they had to be acceptable to Parliament too. And generally speaking that meant that they had to be members of the Commons or the Lords. Crown, government and Parliament had become part of a single system.

This was the 'mixed constitution' of eighteenth-century Britain. It has often been described as corrupt, and it was certainly not democratic. But it made the British system of government very different from the absolute monarchies that ruled most of Europe. This constitution was also a flexible system, able to survive and develop, through all sorts of crises and changes, right up to the present day.

44

Time Line

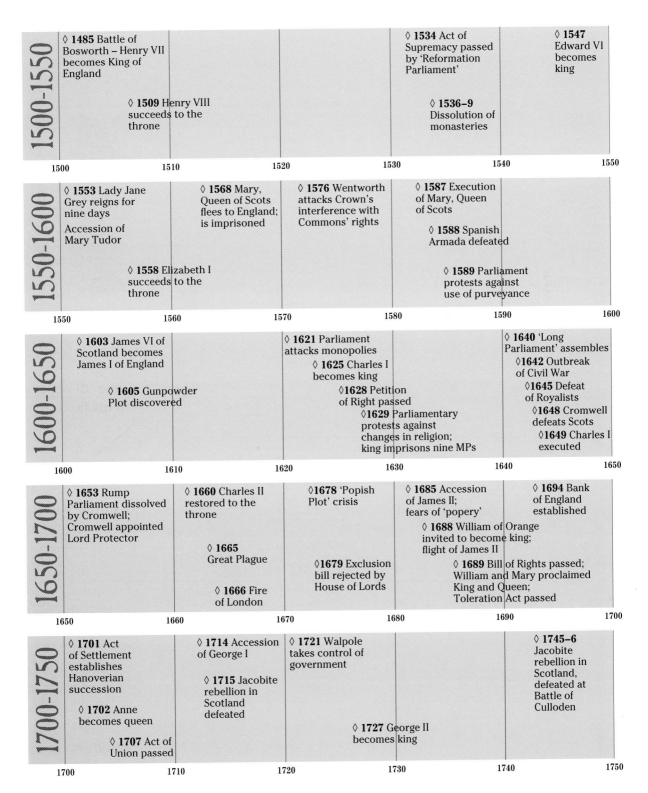

1500-1550

◊ **1485** Battle of Bosworth – Henry VII becomes King of England

◊ **1509** Henry VIII succeeds to the throne

◊ **1534** Act of Supremacy passed by 'Reformation Parliament'

◊ **1536–9** Dissolution of monasteries

◊ **1547** Edward VI becomes king

1500   1510   1520   1530   1540   1550

1550-1600

◊ **1553** Lady Jane Grey reigns for nine days
Accession of Mary Tudor

◊ **1558** Elizabeth I succeeds to the throne

◊ **1568** Mary, Queen of Scots flees to England; is imprisoned

◊ **1576** Wentworth attacks Crown's interference with Commons' rights

◊ **1587** Execution of Mary, Queen of Scots

◊ **1588** Spanish Armada defeated

◊ **1589** Parliament protests against use of purveyance

1550   1560   1570   1580   1590   1600

1600-1650

◊ **1603** James VI of Scotland becomes James I of England

◊ **1605** Gunpowder Plot discovered

◊ **1621** Parliament attacks monopolies
◊ **1625** Charles I becomes king
◊ **1628** Petition of Right passed
◊ **1629** Parliamentary protests against changes in religion; king imprisons nine MPs

◊ **1640** 'Long Parliament' assembles
◊ **1642** Outbreak of Civil War
◊ **1645** Defeat of Royalists
◊ **1648** Cromwell defeats Scots
◊ **1649** Charles I executed

1600   1610   1620   1630   1640   1650

1650-1700

◊ **1653** Rump Parliament dissolved by Cromwell; Cromwell appointed Lord Protector

◊ **1665** Great Plague

◊ **1666** Fire of London

◊ **1660** Charles II restored to the throne

◊ **1678** 'Popish Plot' crisis

◊ **1679** Exclusion bill rejected by House of Lords

◊ **1685** Accession of James II; fears of 'popery'

◊ **1688** William of Orange invited to become king; flight of James II

◊ **1689** Bill of Rights passed; William and Mary proclaimed King and Queen; Toleration Act passed

◊ **1694** Bank of England established

1650   1660   1670   1680   1690   1700

1700-1750

◊ **1701** Act of Settlement establishes Hanoverian succession

◊ **1702** Anne becomes queen

◊ **1707** Act of Union passed

◊ **1714** Accession of George I

◊ **1715** Jacobite rebellion in Scotland defeated

◊ **1721** Walpole takes control of government

◊ **1727** George II becomes king

◊ **1745–6** Jacobite rebellion in Scotland, defeated at Battle of Culloden

1700   1710   1720   1730   1740   1750

Glossary

Abdicate To give up the throne.

Absolute Referring to a king or queen who governs with unrestricted power.

Alliance An agreement made between countries, known as allies, who support each other in certain circumstances.

Assassinated Murdered for political reasons.

Censorship The suppressing of information for political reasons.

Charters Documents recognizing a town's privileges.

Concession Something given in order to make an agreement.

Constitution The set of rules (not necessarily written down) within which a country's political system works.

Dissenters Protestants outside the Church of England.

Divine Right The theory that the monarch is appointed by God, and that opposition is therefore sinful.

Dynasty A sequence of hereditary rulers.

Exile Enforced absence from one's country.

Gentry The landowning classes not counting the nobility.

Henrician Reformation The changes in church government made by Henry VIII.

Jacobites Followers of the exiled Stuarts after James II's flight (1688).

Justices of the Peace (JPs) Local magistrates.

Monopolies Exclusive rights or privileges granted to a person or company. Someone practising such rights is called a monopolist.

Peers Members of the nobility.

Persecuted People ill-treated by others because of their race or religion.

Plague A serious infectious disease, common in Europe between the fourteenth and seventeenth centuries.

Plundering Robbery.

Popery An insulting term for Roman Catholicism.

Prerogative The 'special' rights and powers of the Crown.

Propaganda Ideas spread by bodies such as governments to serve their own interests.

Prorogue To adjourn (end) a session of Parliament.

Puritans Those Protestants who wished to 'purify' the Church of England, removing any remaining traces of Catholicism.

Purveyance The Crown's right to buy provisions below market price.

Reformation A religious and political movement in sixteenth-century Europe, which began as an attempt to reform the Roman Catholic Church and resulted in the establishment of Protestant Churches, including the Church of England.

Republic A form of government without a monarch, usually with an assembly of elected representatives of the people.

Satirical Making fun of a topical issue.

Speaker The presiding officer in the House of Commons.

Statute An Act of Parliament.

Subsidy Taxes voted by Parliament.

Succession The process or right by which one person succeeds to the office of another, for example a king or queen.

Tactic A move or manoeuvre in a struggle.

Toleration Not interfering with the actions, opinions and beliefs of others.

Books to Read

Elizabeth I by Sheila Watson (Wayland, 1995)
Henry VIII by Katrina Siliprandi (Wayland, 1995)
The Jacobites by Iain Rose (Wayland, l995)
James VI/I by K. Kallonatis (Wayland, l995)
The Making of the United Kingdom by Peter Hepplewhite and Neil Tonge (Causeway Press, 1992)

The Stuarts 1603–1714 by Andrew Langley (Hamlyn, 1993)
Tudors by Donna Bailey (Hodder, 1993)
Tudor Monarchs by Jessica Barrauga (Batsford, 1992)
A Wider World – The Making of the United Kingdom by Rosemary Kelly (Stanley Thorne, 1992)

Places of Interest to Visit

The English Civil War Centre
The Commandery
Worcester WR1 2HU.

This half timbered building was the head-quarters of Prince Charles (later Charles II) during the Civil War, before he escaped to France. The centre presents exhibitions telling the story of the Civil War.

Hampton Court Palace
East Molesey
Surrey KT8 9AU.

The building of this Thameside palace was begun by Cardinal Wolsey in 1514. It became a royal palace when Henry VIII acquired it and added to the building.

Later additions were made for William III by the architect Sir Christopher Wren. The palace houses notable collections of furniture, tapestries and paintings of the period 1500–1750.

National Portrait Gallery
St Martins Place
London WC2H 0HE.

The collection includes portraits of many of the monarchs and other important figures of the period.

Royal Museum of Scotland
Queen Street
Edinburgh EH2 1JD.

Contains collections of Stuart relics, Highland weapons, costumes and textiles.

Tower of London
Tower Hill
London EC3N 4AB.

This fortress has been a state prison since Norman times and is the scene of many celebrated executions. The Crown Jewels and Regalia are displayed in the Wakefield Tower and the White Tower contains the National Collection of Arms and Armour.

Index